Happy New Year, Alison
Fondest Love
Mum, 1984.

Lys de Bray

Midsummer Silver

J. M. Dent & Sons Ltd
London Melbourne Toronto

First published 1980

Printed in Great Britain by
Biddles Ltd Guildford Surrey
for J. M. Dent & Sons Ltd
Aldine House Welbeck Street London

This book is set in 11pt Apollo

British Library Cataloguing in Publication Data

de Bray, Lys
Midsummer silver.
1. Plants, Useful
I. Title
581.6′1 QK98.4

ISBN 0-460-04512-1

Contents

By the same author

The Wild Garden

Foreword

I have called this book 'Midsummer Silver', which is the beautiful name of a little yellow wild flower with shimmering silver leaves. For me this flower symbolizes hot summer, narrow dusty country roads, blue skies, lark song and the scent of gorse on a hillside. It is one of a collection of flowery snippets in this book – light as flummery – which ideally should be read in a looped and tasselled hammock, gently swinging in the dappled shade of old orchard Apple trees. The book is just the right length to be assimilated before dozing pleasantly off to sleep.

Most of the flowers and trees that I have written about are old friends, and so they were to our ancestors who used them to comfort their souls, heal their wounds and mend their hearts; so the book contains remedies which will work, but add patience to the list of ingredients. Your own pot-pourri from your own garden is much better than any that you can buy, because the flowers are those that you have sown, grown and known. There are hundreds more equally practical plants for other practical purposes. Everyone needs just a little better luck than they have, which is why most of the spells in this book are charms of love – try them and see, and it may be that we shall have a kinder world.

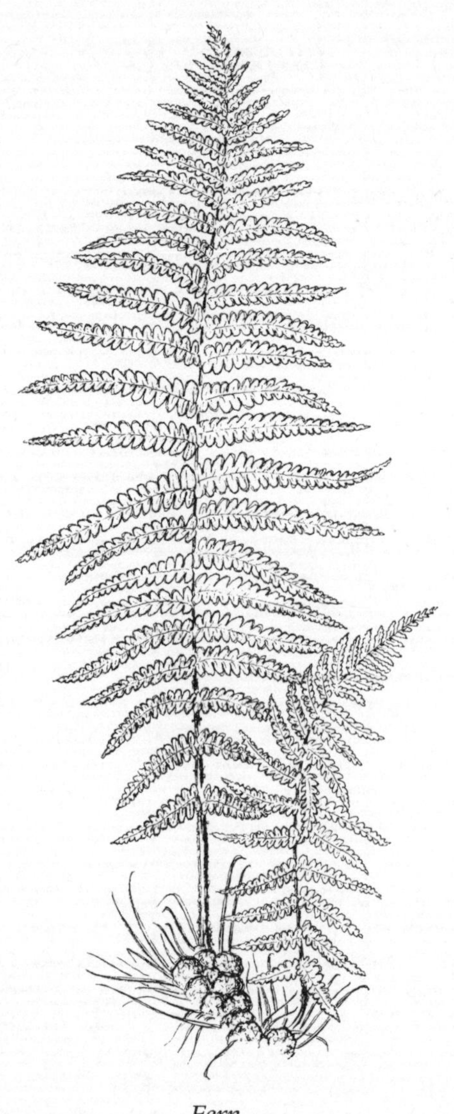

Fern

1 Summer Magic

Magic was believed in during the Middle Ages because, as far as people knew, it had always been there. Powers for good and bad, black and white, were attributed to almost anyone who stood apart either in appearance, behaviour or habitation. A belief in magic was an early form of positive thinking, and if one believed hard enough that a certain thing would happen – it very often did. The many love-charms and spells that have come down to us speak very positively of Everyman's desire, then as now, to be wanted and to be saved from evil or plain bad luck.

Being practical, our forebears took steps to see that they achieved their desires by any means possible, and there is a great legacy from those former centuries which may be believed or taken with a pinch of salt – and that is yet another superstition . . .

Fern Seed

To become invisible

It is said that if Fern seed is worn about the person the cloak of invisibility can be donned at will. The seed has to be that of the Male Fern, and it can be sought only on St John's Eve (June 23rd). If the proper ceremonial is not observed while gathering the seed, it will often vanish while being carried home. Fern seed was used with other equally magical ingredients to make the legendary witches' 'flying ointment' – a salve that incorporated Hellebore, Hemlock and Aconite among other less savoury ingredients.

Vervain

For love-charms and protection

Vervain is an insignificant wild flower that can grow to a height of about three feet; it has small mauve-blue flowers and rather dusty-looking leaves, and is easily passed by in a hedgerow. For hundreds of years it was regarded as a herb of healing and love, and part of a very old charm to be said while gathering it is repeated here:

All hele, thou holy herb Vervin,
Growing on the ground;
In the mount of Calvery
There was thou found;
Thou helpest many a greife,
And Stenchest many a wound.
In the name of sweet Jesus,
I take thee from the ground.
Oh, Lord, effect the same
That I do go about.
In the name of God, on Mount Olivet
First I thee found;
In the name of Jesus
I pull thee from the ground.

Vervain was used as a holy herb of protection against evil enchantments, and a rhyme of that period was:

Vervain and Dill
Hinder witches from their will.

A simple love-charm from a sixteenth-century collection ran as follows: 'Rubbe vervin in the bale of thy hande and rubbe thy mouth with it and immediatelye kysse her and it is done.'

Couch Grass

To entrance the hearer

This indestructible grass of the running roots had a useful reputation for spellbinding audiences. The instructions were as follows: just before dawn, go to where the Couch grass grows, and pull up some of its roots, saying meanwhile 'As the birds wake and sing, so will I wake and sing; as we listen to them so they listen to me'. Then wash the roots in running water and eat them. This to be done three mornings in succession during the waxing moon. For any person who made his living by oratory and who doubted his own powers, perhaps a little magic of this kind helped to 'Entrance the hearers'.

Apple

For divination

Apple skins are used for simple divination, and schoolgirls still drop the long uncut peeled skin of an apple on the ground to see what letter of the alphabet it forms; the letter will be the initial of the man the girl will marry. Boys at this age are somewhat less interested in thoughts of matrimony, usually preferring the practising of martial arts.

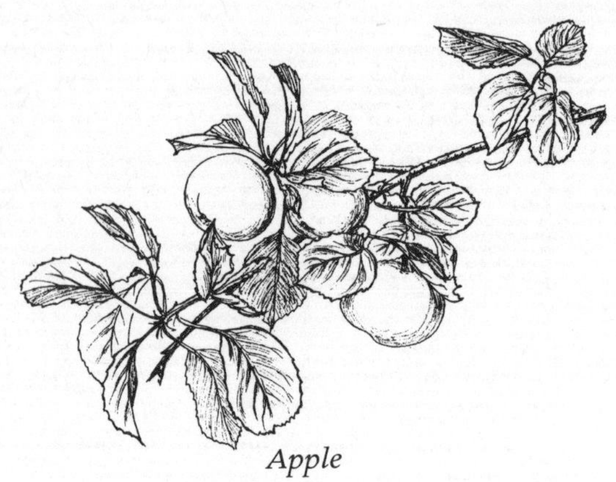

Apple

It was said to be unlucky to fall asleep under an Apple tree, because the fairies might carry you away; this is understandable when sleeping beneath the sinister and funereal Cypress, but it is difficult to believe that an honest Apple tree could ever have any part in bad luck, though Apples themselves have a history of usefulness in magic, both bad and good, and an example of this is seen in the story of Snow White and the Seven Dwarfs.

There is an old love-spell which makes one reluctant to receive an Apple as a gift ever again: 'Take an Apple in thy hande as it hangeth on the tree and wryte in it these names followinge. *Anaell, Satnell, Asiell* & then saye I coniure thee Apple of Apples by the name of cheefe devels, which decetpfully deceaved Eve in padyce, that what woman soever it be that doe eate or tast of this Apple that she may burne in love of me. Saye this 4 tymes upon the Apple, & then geve the Apple to what woman you will.'

Bindweed

A binding spell

Bindweed lives up to its name, and can be used to make your proposed victim do what you will. The spell must be performed during the three days before new moon, and firstly you must make a puppet or image in anything malleable such as dough or mud. This must be baptized in the name of the person to be bewitched, and bound nine times with a length

Bindweed

of the stem of the Bindweed – (nine revolutions round anti-clockwise) while saying 'I bind (Name) against or to (whatever action is wanted or not wanted) So shall it be'. Then bury the puppet or image in a path where the person is sure to walk.

Periwinkle

For love between man and wife

The pretty purple Periwinkle was formerly called 'Sorcerer's Violet' and it has had a part in very many traditions both bad, sad and rather unpleasant. An old love-charm is described as follows: 'Perwynke when it is beate unto pouder with worms of ye earth wrapped about it and with an herbe called houselyke, it induceth love between man and wyfe if it bee used in their meales.'

Periwinkle

Onion

A way to know whom you shall marry

'Take an Onion called St Thomas's Onion, peel it and put it into a clean handkerchief, put on a clean smock, and lay it under your head (the handkerchief) have the room clean swept then lie down and spreading your Arms abroad say:

St Thomas, pray do me Right
And let my True Love come tonight
That I may behold his face
And him in my kind Arms Embrace.

Then fall asleep, and in your dreams you shall see him come to you, be not Coy, but get hold of him and then you will be sure 'tis he, but if he gives you the slip try again.'

Daisy

To take fish

'Take the roote of a daisy & franchensent & beat them small together & temper it with manisy it will be like salve or gum & keep it in a boxe & you will Anoynt your bayte or fly when you fysh they will com to it.'

Egg

Another love spell

'Laye an Egge in a pismyre banke (Ant's nest) ye 18 days of March, & lett it lye ther 3 dayes then take it out & whosoever thou touchest with yt shall Love thee.'

Scarlet Pimpernel

To hear birds and animals talking

This little flower likes to be sure about the quality of the new day before it opens, so the tiny red petals often remain closed until after eight in the morning, even in midsummer. It was considered to be a magical flower, and, if held in the hand, it gave you the power to hear and understand the speech of birds and animals.

Agrimony

To induce sleep

The thin yellow flower-spikes of Agrimony flourish among the grasses beside many a country road. For hundreds of years this plant has had magical associations, and one use for it was to induce deep sleep. This rhyme from the eleventh century instructs:

If it be leyd under mann's heed
He shal sleepyn as he were deed,
He shal never drede ne wakyn
Till from under his heed it be takyn.

Burdock

A love-potion

A powerful love-potion may be made with the hooked seed-heads. These should be pounded in a mortar and mixed with the private parts of a billy-goat and some hairs from a white puppy which should be cut on the first day of the new moon and burnt on the seventh. To this mixture add some brandy and leave in a quiet place quite uncovered for it to be impregnated with the astral influences. After this the compound should be cooked until it is thick, adding a few drops of crocodile sperm.

The difficulty of obtaining some of the ingredients will limit the general use of this recipe.

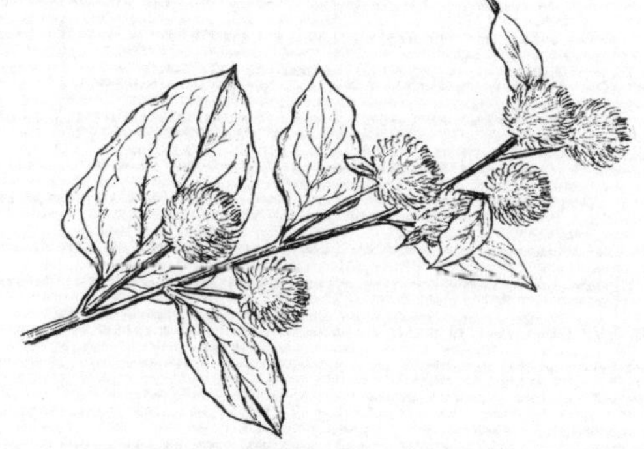

Burdock

2 Flowers of Fortune

Some plants' associations are so firmly rooted in dim history that we know them simply as 'bad' or 'good' without knowing exactly why. The reasons for this probably date back to the days of the Pharaohs, and certainly to Roman times, when most plants had special associations with Gods and Goddesses, who in their turn were either good and were rewarded or evil and had to be placated. The fascinating mythology has been forgotten but a memory or two remains from our own childhood when we were taken for a walk in the country, and old legends of this or that plant were told to us to keep us amused by someone old enough to remember the tales of our great-grandparents.

Holly
(Ilex aquifolium)

Holly is a good-luck tree in every way, particularly as it has red berries; the colour red wards off the evil eye. A Holly tree planted near the house will protect both it and all who dwell therein from ill luck and against lightning. A young tree should not be planted under the overhang of the eaves, where it will not get enough water, and in any case the roots would eventually damage the foundations of the house; from ten to fifteen feet is 'near' enough to be both sensible and beneficial.

Holly

One curiosity about modern nomenclature is that the variegated holly called 'Golden Queen' is a male plant, and the variety 'Golden King' is a female. Both need a friend of the opposite sex to be planted nearby for cross-pollination and the resultant berries.

Rowan

(Sorbus aucuparia)

When I was a child I was told to sew a piece of Rowan tree into the hems of my dresses (to keep the witches away) and the little twigs must have been a bumpy curiosity to whoever did the ironing. This is another good-luck tree, red-berried for protection against all bad magic. A Rowan tree is always beautiful, with the creamy plates of flowers in the spring or the scarlet berries of autumn set among bright green ferny leaves. It was always a tree of good luck and protection against the evil eye, and its wood was once carefully carved into horse-harness as a prevention against accidents.

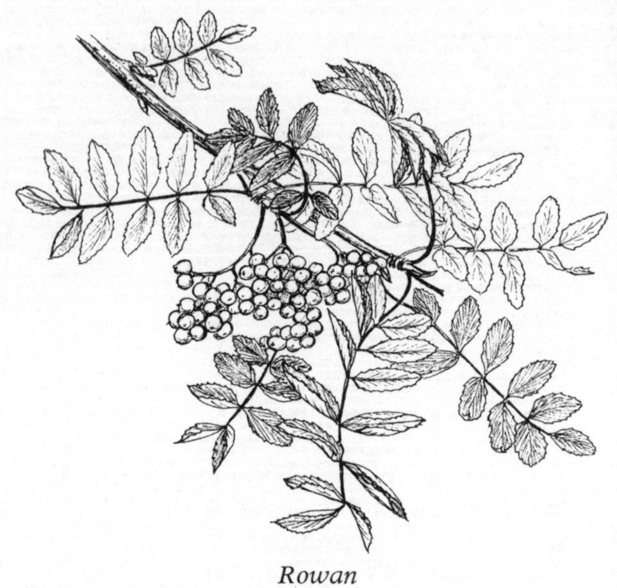

Rowan

Elder

(Sambucus nigra)

An Elder tree is a wicked tree and no part of it brings luck though, strangely, there is nothing wrong with the fruit or flowers which have numerous medicinal uses.

There are many damning beliefs about the wood of the tree, and it will bring bad luck to any house if it be burnt in the fireplace. No piece of the wood should ever be used in the building of boats, and furniture should never be made of it, least of all a baby's cradle.

When hearses were horse-drawn, the drivers would choose a whip-handle made of

Elder wood to protect themselves against the spirit of the newly-dead still floating close to its earthly clay, particularly so if the passing were violent or tragic. Another death-superstition was that he who had an Elder tree in his garden would die in his own bed.

There is a rankness surrounding an Elder bush, and nothing will grow in its shadow. This therefore is an excellent place for a compost-heap, because the roots of the tree excrete a substance which will hasten fermentation in the heap, and the compost will itself enrich the tree.

Elder Fruit

White Bryony, English Mandrake
(Brionia dioica)

This is a very pretty – though poisonous – plant of the hedgerow, with its pale green palmate leaves, spiralling tendrils and sprays of cream-green flowers accompanied by green

White Bryony

berries which later turn to orange and red. This is the English equivalent of the Mandrake, though its root is more turnip- than parsnip-shaped. Unscrupulous apothecaries of former times carved it into man-shaped figures and sold it as true Mandrake root to barren women anxious to conceive. Not a lucky plant – it must have been the cause of many a disappointment.

Bittersweet, Woody Nightshade
(Solanum dulcamara)

Another strong character in the Nightshade family, this member of it brought good fortune and protection against witchcraft. Bittersweet is a scrambling plant of hedge and seashore, with dangling violet and yellow flowers; it is often mistakenly called 'Deadly Nightshade', and, though its red berries are poisonous, they are not so terminal as the shining, cherry-sized black fruits of *Atropa bella-donna,* the true Deadly Nightshade.

When sheep and cattle were cared for by herdsmen, twisted garlands of Bittersweet were hung around the animal's necks as an amulet against their being 'overlooked'. This belief in the efficacy of the plant as a protector carries back thousands of years – when the tomb of Tutankhamen was discovered and opened, dried Bittersweet berries were found, worked into a jewelled collar, as part of the luck-bringing grave furniture.

Moon-Daisy, Ox-eye Daisy

(Chrysanthemum leucanthemum)

Moon-daisies look like smaller and more delicate Marguerites and were always regarded as luck-bringing flowers of protection, particularly in Europe. Used with other flowers in the St John's Eve garlands, Moon-daisies were thought to have sovereign powers against lightning – an old English name for them was 'Thunder Daisy'. The flowers were hung up in hay-lofts and on hay-ricks as a protection,

Moon-Daisy

because rick fires, with a consequent shortage of winter fodder, meant certain death for the farmer's beasts in the longer winters of those days.

Gorse, Whin

(Ulex europaeus)

Gorse is triumphantly in flower the whole year round – and the old saying, 'Kissing's out of season when the Gorse is out of bloom' reflects the dry humour of the practical countryman. Gorse is a good-luck flower (unless brought indoors, when it meant a certain death in the house) and an old Irish traveller's custom was to wear a sprig of Gorse in the hat to preserve weary feet from stumbling.

Gorse

Red Campion

(Melandrium rubrum)

A bad plant, associated with the Devil and Robin Goodfellow who was a kind of chancy-tempered wood-goblin, sometimes benevolent but more often not. Pink flowers of spring (like Herb-Robert) were unlucky, and many May-blooming flowers had particular significance for good or evil.

Red Campion is not to be confused with Ragged Robin, whose petals are the same colour but are forked into little twisting tails; Ragged Robin thrives only in damp pastures and ditches, whereas the Red Campion is equally happy in a Bluebell wood or on a sunny hedge-bank. Picking the flowers of Red Campion with the appropriate conjuration could (if all were done correctly and in order), be the means of cursing the picker's father who would inevitably die. White Campion worked in the same way on the maternal side. Many of the other country names for this flower have the word 'Robin' in them, e.g. Robin's Eye, Robin-run-in-the-hedge, Robin's Flower, Red Robin, etc. and this meant that the Robin of our gardens was thought to be as unlucky as the flower.

Hawthorn, May, Quickthorn

(Crataegus monogyna)

The most protective and lucky flower of all – but only outside and in the open air. It was woven into prickly garlands for the May-Pole,

Hawthorn

because everything green and growing needed extra protection and blessings during the month of May. In former days the month of May was warmer than it is now (the calendar was changed in 1732) and so the May tree would have been in full flower much earlier in the month; today, except in the western counties, the May will not be in bloom until nearer the middle of the month.

Because the tree was held in such respect in the open air, it was, and still is, considered the most unlucky flower possible to gather for vases in the house – whether it be the wild White Quickthorn of the hedge, the May bush standing alone with its sheep-rubbed trunk, or the double red May of suburban avenues.

Arum Lily

(Zantedeschia aethiopica)

This beautiful lily is regarded with intense dislike by many people, who say – 'Ah, funerals!' when they see it; it is not a flower to give as a gift, because it usually symbolizes formal altar-pieces at Easter, or religious illustration and embroideries. Its waxy white scrolls are certainly seen in many church flower arrangements, but this is often because of the flower's purity of shape and long-lasting properties. It also happens to flower at Easter, though the fine clumps seen growing in cottage gardens in Cornwall come into bloom a month later. It grows well in ponds and can be left out all winter if the tubers are deep enough.

Arum Lily

3 *Pot-pourri*

In former times, though it was not particularly fashionable to wash, it was certainly essential to be expensively perfumed. Bad smells, and there must have been many, were cloaked and masked by sweet, heavy scents, and it was as natural for a court gentleman to wear perfume as it was for his lady. The art of the perfumer would need to have been, therefore, a little heavy handed in the atmosphere of the conflicting stenches that were taken for granted.

Many people in the country – and there was much more of it then – made their own perfumes as a matter of course, because the raw materials were all around them, as they still are today. Great houses and small manors had still-rooms for the production of the year's preserves, and the art of distillation was known to far more people then than today. Such soap as was used was made at home in vast quantities for a year's use, and much more was known about the niceties of the blending and balance of flower-scents.

Some of the essential ingredients they used, such as Musk, Civet and Ambergris were expensively obtained from the Far Eastern traders in the then unlimited sources of the wild. There are modern substitutes for these ingredients now, which may be obtained easily from specialist shops found in the large capital cities of the world. The flowers and leaves are already there in our gardens, and could so easily give us an exquisite memory of summer during the short dark days of winter.

Properly made pot-pourri will last for several years if it is kept in a closed container as was originally intended. The following recipe was one of many that were used, and though the quantities for today's needs should be decreased, it is very important to keep the proportions the same.

A Recipe for Pot-pourri

'Put into a large China jar the following ingredients in layers with bay-salt strewed between the layers: two pecks of damask-roses, part in bud and part blown; violets, orange-flowers, and jasmine, a handful of each; orris-root sliced, benjamin and storax, two ounces of each; a quarter of an ounce of musk; a quarter of a pound of angelica-root sliced; two handsful of lavender-flowers; half a handful of rosemary-flowers; bay and laurel leaves, half a

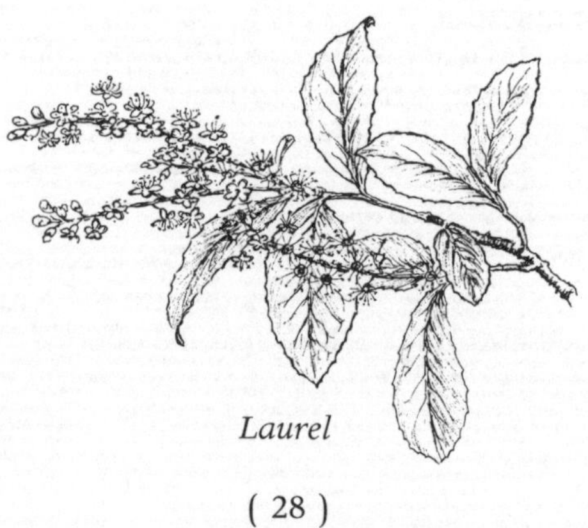

Laurel

Rosemary and Lavender

handful of each; three Seville oranges, stuck as full of cloves as possible, dried in a cool oven, and pounded; half a handful of knotted marjoram; and two handsful of balm of Gilead dried. Coverall quite close. When the pot is uncovered, the perfume is very fine.'

Domestic Cookery (1834)

Rosemary was a very important plant in the gardens of the Middle Ages, particularly during the time of the plàgues, because it was thought to be a most effective prophylactic. During the reign of Charles II when the Great Plague was at its height, small sprigs of Rosemary were sold in the streets at the inflated price of sixpence each, whereas in previous years a herb-woman's whole armful was worth but twelve pence; rising prices owing to shortages were as prevalent then as now. The following recipes use Rosemary generously:

Odoriferous Water

'Take sweet Basil, Mint, sweet Marjoram, Florentine Orrice-root, Hyssop, Balm, Savory, Lavender, and Rosemary, of each a handful; Cloves, Cinnamon, and Nutmegs, of each half an ounce; three or four Lemons, cut in thick slices; infuse them three days in a good quantity of Rose-water; distil in a water bath with a gentle fire, and add to the distilled water a scruple of Musk.'

The Toilet of Flora

Hungary Water

'To one pint of highly rectified spirit of wine, put an ounce of oil of rosemary, and two drachms of essence of ambergris; shake the bottle several times, then let the cork remain out twenty-four hours. After a month, during which time shake it daily, put the water into small bottles.'

Domestic Cookery (1834)

The art of the medieval perfumer was not as sophisticated in England as it was in France, where the first charter was granted to the perfume-makers in the twelfth century. In Elizabeth I's reign, one of the most popular scents was simple Rose-water, which was used on its own (see the following recipe) or as a base for many other purposes.

Rose

Rose-water

'Some do put rose-water in a glass and they put roses with their dew thereto and they make it to boile in water thā thei set it in the sune tyll it be readde and this water is beste.

Also drye roses put to the nose to smell do comforte the braine and the harte and quencheth spirits.'

Askham's Herbal (1550)

This recipe uses Rose-water as a base:

To make a speciall sweet water to perfume clothes in the folding being washed

'Take a quart of Damaske-Rose-Water and put it into a glasse, put unto it a handfull of Lavender Flowers, two ounces of Orris, a dram of Muske, the weight of four pence of Ambergreece, as much Civet, foure drops of Oyle of Cloves, stop this close, and set it in the Sunne a fortnight; put one spoonful of this Water into a bason of common water and put it into a glasse and so sprinkle your clothes therewith in your folding: the dregs, left in the bottome (when the water is spent) will make as much more, if you keepe them, and put fresh Rose-water to it.'

Sir Hugh Platt, *Delights for Ladies* (1594)

Rose-water was used to wash the hands after banquets because there was as yet no cutlery: food was cut up with a knife, impaled on the point and so transferred to the mouth by the daintier guests at the board (most people used their fingers). Napkins and bowls of Rose-water, therefore, were an essential termination of any feast.

The following recipe for a seventeenth-century toilet-water is full of scented delight, though the 'wild dasie' would have had a quicker effect on skin blemishes used as a plain poultice.

An excellent water to clear Hands and Face

'Take a quart of fair water, a pint of white wine, the juice of 4 lemons: put into these bean blossoms, elder blossoms, white lily blossoms,

White Lily

a handful of them all: put amongst the wine and water and put into 4 wild dasie roots, 4 marsh mallow roots and 2 or 3 bunches of wild tansie, as much of fumitary, the weight of 2 pence in camphere: put all these together in an earthen pot, set the pot in warm aishes all night, then in the morning strain it through a piece of white cotton clean wash'd and put it into a narrow mouth glass: sit the glass in the sun 3 or 4 days in the heat of the sun. Wash your face with this water evening and morning. If you wash your hands with any of this water put thereto 3 or 4 bruised almonds, this is the most excellent water that ever was made to clear hands and face withall. Probatum est.'

The Book of Simples (circa 1650)

Pomanders were made as hard balls which were threaded on a cord and carried about to ward off infections and 'pestilential airs'. Sometimes the pomander was left as it was, though more often it was put into a valuable pierced box of ivory, silver or gold, and carried as a fashionable ornament of dress.

An excellent Pomander

'Take half an ounce of benjamin, half an ounce of Damask rose leaves, a quarter of an ounce of Storax: beat these very small severally, then sift them and mingle the powder: then take some gumdragon steep'd in rose water 24 hours and make it into a stiff paste: then take 4 grains of ambergreese, 4 grains of musk and 2 of civit: grind these together with a little juice of Lemon till they are dissolved: then anoint the hand with essence of jessamie or roses and work the past well with the musk and amber: if it be too limber put in powder of roses, if too stiff, a little rose water, then weigh and rowle them up in your hand, but while they are wet make holes through them with a bodkin: Dry them betwixt 2 papers.'

The Book of Simples (circa 1650)

To renew the scent of a Pomander

'Take one grain of Civet, and two of Musk, or if you double the Proportion it will be so much the sweeter: grinde them upon a stone with a little Rose-water, and after, wetting your hands with Rose-water, you may worke the same in your Pomander. This is a sleight to pass away an old Pomander: but my intention is honest.'

Sir Hugh Platt, *Delights for Ladies* (1594)

Today, pomanders can be made and hung in wardrobes and clothes-closets; the great plagues of the past are gone for ever, but we still have *Tineola bisselliela*, the clothes-moth, which can be defeated by a sweet smell.

Perfumes were once made to be burned, which was almost a necessity in some medieval houses, particularly in a sick-room. Windows were never opened during a period of illness – the unknown evil demons lurking without would have flown in immediately and further possessed the soul and body of the invalid. The following recipes would have been quite effective in these circumstances.

A very good Perfume to burn

'Take two Ounces of the Powder of Juniper Wood, one Ounce of Benjamin, one Ounce of Storax, six drops of oil of Limons, as much oil of Cloves, ten grains of Musk, six of Civet, mould them up with a little gum-Dragon steeped in Rosewater, make them in little Cakes and dry them between Rose leaves, your Juniper wood must be well dried, beaten and searced.'

The Queen's Closet Opened (1662)

To make a Perfume to burn in a Chamber

'Take Benjamine, Storax and Labdanum, of each a little; a little damaske powder, orace powder, a little, a little frankincense and mirr, powder of Jniper; beat all these together to a paste in a hot morter and so make it up in the fashion of great black cloves and so burn them when you please, it's a pleasant smell.'

The Book of Simples (circa 1650)

A bath can be a necessity, a benison for aching bones, or a perfumed indulgence. Baths should be sybaritic, beneficial or beautifying and, though they were not indulged in too often in former days, some recipes have been passed down to us which indicate that the period between the decline of the Roman Empire and the present day was not entirely a dark time of barbarianism.

A Cosmetic Bath

'Take two pounds of Barley or Bean-meal, eight pounds of Bran, and a few handfuls of Borage leaves. Boil these ingredients in a sufficient quantity of spring water. Nothing cleanses and softens the skin like this bath.'

The Toilet of Flora

To make a bath for Melancholy

'Take Mallowes, pellitory of the wall, of each three handfulls; Camomell flowers, Mellilot flowers of each one handfull; hollyhocks, two handfulls; Isop one greate handfull, senerick seede one ounce, and boil them in nine gallons of water untill they come to three, then put in a quart of new milke and go into it bloud warm or something warmer.' *Arcana Fairfaxiana*

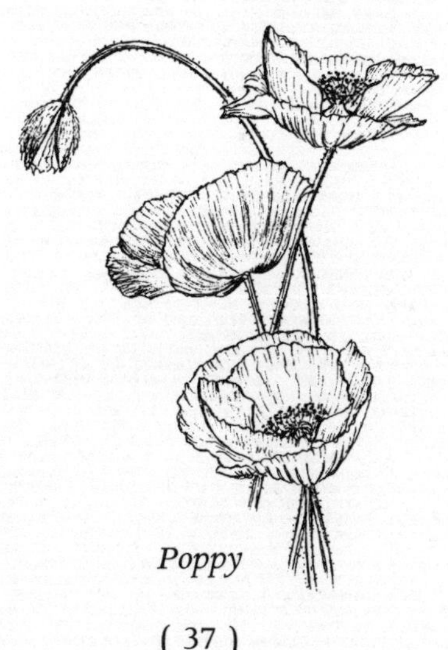

Poppy

For an aphrodisiac bath

For a bath that is reputed to have the same effect on the libido as rhinocerous horn, the following recipe should be tried: mix equal quantities by weight of the following plants, either fresh or dried. Field Poppy, True Valerian, Pansy, Periwinkle, Maidenhair Fern and Male Fern. Sprinkle one ounce of this mixture on to two pints of cold water and bring to the boil; simmer for a few minutes. Remove from heat and allow to cool, strain and add the liquid to warm bath-water.

Bluebell

4 Healing Herbs

Our forefathers were skilled at curing the ailments, illnesses and wounds of the times. They used the natural remedies known and proved by *their* fathers, or they went to the monasteries whose enclosed herb-gardens were the source of most of the known medicine of medieval times. Many people today are cautiously beginning to experiment with herbal medicine, and they are finding that, though the ultimate cure takes far longer to achieve in many cases, there are no cumulative and deleterious side-effects caused by the instant, and powerful – though often inadequately researched – modern wonder-drugs.

Silverweed

(Potentilla anserina)

Silverweed – or Midsummer Silver – was much loved and very much more appreciated by our forefathers, who carved its formalized shape on pew-ends in their churches in lasting tribute to its beauty and its usefulness. Another of its pretty names is 'Goose Grey' because geese like it so much, while the foot-travellers of yester-year called it 'Traveller's Ease' for they could always be sure of finding it growing by the edge of the road, where they would stop and gather a handful of cool leaves to line their worn boots for comfort and to prevent soreness. This little yellow flower with the beautiful leaves is well named, because it is potent in herbal medicine. It can soothe sore throats, heal wounds, ease menstrual pains, cure diarrhoea and clear adolescent skins of pimples, which, when one is sixteen and in love, is important above everything.

If Midsummer Silver were a delicate alpine, it would be cherished and coveted, but its silver-white leaves seem able to thrive in appallingly dry and inhospitable conditions, where its strong runners are quite capable of producing acres of shimmering beauty.

Blackberry
(Rubus fruticosus)

Blackberry leaves contain styptic properties, and curiously therefore, may be used to staunch the bleeding scratches suffered while

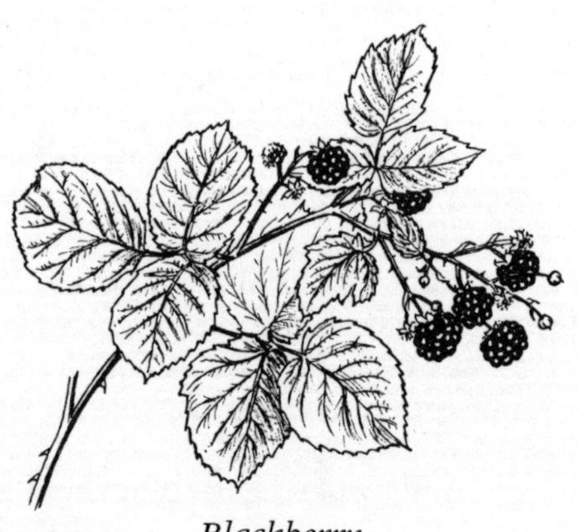

Blackberry

picking Blackberries from the bush you were scratched by. Crush up some clean fresh leaves and use them as a compress to arrest the flow of blood. This same compress is soothing for insect bites and burns.

Comfrey

(Symphytum officinale)

So much has been written about Comfrey that the considerable therapeutic powers of this plant can only be touched on here. It has been used medicinally for over 2000 years, and in the Middle Ages it was, and still is, called 'Knitbone' or 'Boneset' because it was believed to have an almost magical capability to join broken bones together again. Modern herbalists still use compresses of the grated root to heal obstinate varicose ulcers, because the root has been found to contain allantoin which stimulates the healthy granulation of tissue, and it is one of the few plants which can manufacture vitamin B^{12}.

Teas, tinctures, infusions, decoctions and extracts of Comfrey are still being used to cure or at least alleviate an incredible list of ailments, such as whooping cough, catarrh, laryngitis, bronchitis, quinsy, diarrhoea, dysentery, enteritis, stomach ulcers, phlebitis, erysipelas, gout, haemorrhoids, burns, scalds and bad bruising. In the Middle Ages the list was even longer and much more comprehensive, for it then included agues, sharpness of humours, running ulcers, gangrenes, mortification and consumption.

Comfrey

Marigold

(Calendula officinalis)

This is the ordinary cottage garden Marigold, which has been used as a harmless food-colouring for hundreds of years because it is readily available and cheap, compared to the rare and expensive Saffron. The flowers are still made into an ointment which will heal small wounds without a scar, and the chopped-up fresh plant applied as a simple compress will soothe burns and scalds. The juice from the cut stem will cure small warts, if it is applied regularly.

Marigold

Sunflower

(Helianthus annua)

Smiling Sunflowers in a row are a traditional sight in a cottage garden – and they can never be persuaded to all grow to the same height. They must face south to give of their best, and their amiable faces will follow the sun all day, finally gazing into the western skies in the evening. By the morning they will have turned back, ready to greet the sun's coming in the east, and they will repeat the process day after day, like a vegetable satellite tracking station.

Sunflower

Their enormous friendly faces are packed full of useful goodness; indeed, every part of the plant has some economic value. The leaves are used as cattle fodder, and the thick, hairy stems have been successfully made into paper but it is the huge 'plate' of seeds which is so rich in valuable and nutritious oil. Sunflower seeds have been used for many years in alleviating coughs, colds, laryngitis and bronchial complaints.

Elder

(Sambucus nigra)

The tree itself has a sinister and evil reputation, but this does not carry over to the fruit or flowers. The creamy blossom can be used for many scented delights which have a very practical purpose, such as Elderflower water, Elderflower cream, baths, teas, wine and a vinegar. The flowers can be eaten as fritters, but it is not wise to over-indulge because they will have the same rapid effect as too many green figs. Though the blossom itself – when sniffed – has a slightly musky smell, all the various products that can be made from it lose this muskiness during the various processes of heating, and there is left a delicious, light summery fragrance. Elderflower water is a gentle and natural astringent (which will clear freckles), the cream is good for rough skin, the bath is refreshing and will whiten and soften the skin, the tea is good for colds and chills, and Elderflower vinegar is a panacea for sore throats.

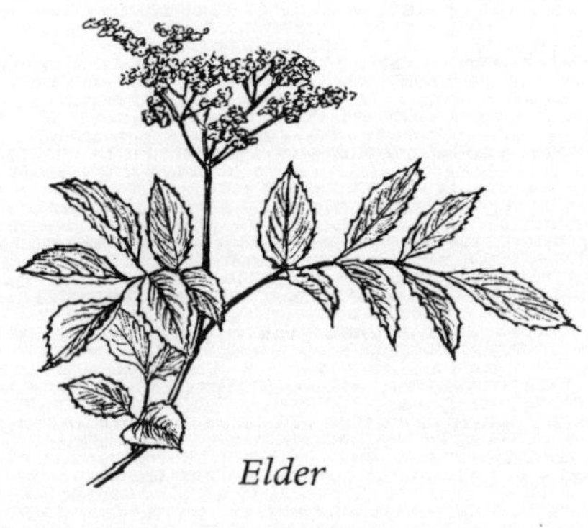

Elder

Duckweed

(Lemna minor)

The familiar light green skin of Duckweed that is so often seen on still water is part of that water's health cycle: not only is it food for ducks and other waterfowl, but it is an oxygenating agent and a cover for fish to skulk under. In addition to these functions it may be made into a tisane to alleviate catarrh, but be sure to take the Duckweed from an unpolluted pond.

Tansy

(Tanacetum vulgare)

Tansy is another medicinal plant introduced to this country by monks in the Middle Ages. Medieval stomachs must have been a great deal stronger than our over-delicate interiors, because varying measures of the plant were used as a flavouring (for Tansy cakes at Easter), as a powerful vermifuge, as a diuretic, to procure abortions (and, curiously, a potion of Tansy, boiled in beer, was thought to prevent miscarriages). An earlier use for the plant was as a strewing herb because its aromatic, camphor-scented leaves were very effective as a flea-repellent.

Today's use for this very ornamental and historical plant is to keep ants out of the larder; leaves placed round the windowsill will, especially if mixed with those of Mint, act as an effective deterrent if you cannot bear to pour boiling water on the invisible nests; the herbs

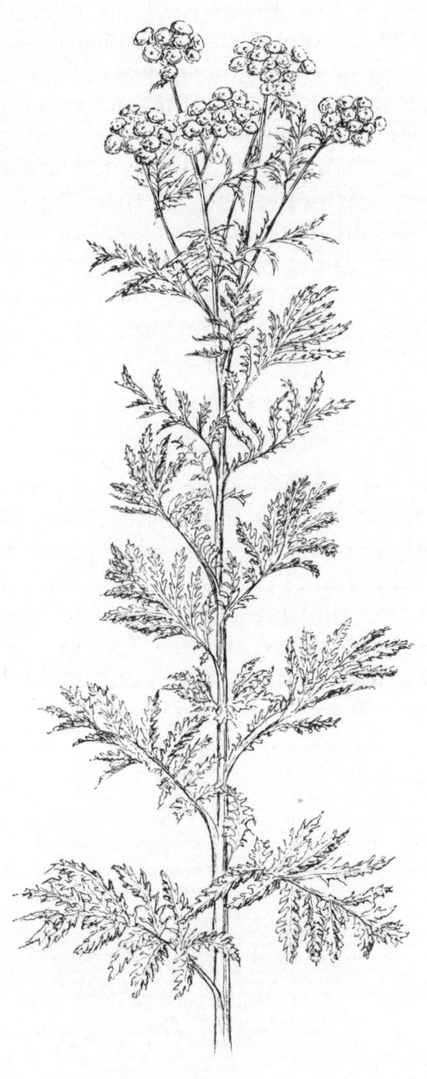

Tansy

are safer in the larder than the other alternative of leaving trails of chemical warfare near food, or where the animals of the house may get it on their feet if the ant's entry-point is under the kitchen door. Better still, grow Tansy and Mint together under the larder – or kitchen – window and let them fight each other for survival; each is about as strong as the other. Today's research has proved that Tansy contains a volatile oil (Thujone) of which an overdose can be fatal.

Plantain

(Plantago major)

Plague of perfectionist lawn-keepers, the plate-flat Plantain is an historical herb of healing. Alone or mixed with other plants it has been valued since earliest man first cut himself on his first flint knife. The (washed) crushed leaves are a cooling poultice for cuts, grazes, bruises, insect stings, burns and scalds. The Saxons called it 'Weybroed' and used it for all

Plantain

their external hurts. It travelled – as seed – to all parts of the New World then being discovered and young plants appeared wherever the pioneers had passed; the Red Indians called it 'White Man's Foot' because the flat leaf rosettes sprang up as if by magic in the wagon-tracks of the early settlers.

Dog Rose

(Rosa canina)

The fragile delicacy of a branch of Wild Roses is one of the loveliest sights of the countryside in June, and the flowers have a light fragrance that matches their pale beauty. Later on in the

Wild Rose

weak autumn sunshine, sprays of ruby hips will glow in place of the flowers against the sombre setting of the November hedgerow; the jewel-like quality of the hips is not confined to their appearance alone, because each hip is a little treasure-chest of usefulness.

The hips consist of a fleshy wall which is the receptacle for the downy seeds. The down itself is a harmless vermifuge, the dried, powdered seeds an old cure for colic, and the receptacle when dried correctly yields more Vitamin C than the same weight of Lemons or Oranges. A tisane can be prepared from the dried hips (first removing the downy seeds) which is, for once, a pleasant-tasting remedy for fatigue and spring lassitude. Rose-hip jam tastes delicious and is a gentle remedy for diarrhoea.

Dock

(Rumex acetosa)

My wonderful old gardener, stronger and fitter at seventy-six than I ever was at forty, has a number of effective country cures. For a friend with boils, he gathers dock roots from our unpolluted field (very important, these days) and takes them home and scrubs them; then he puts the roots in a big old saucepan with enough water to cover them, and they are simmered until they are soft, depending on how large the roots are. The potful is allowed to cool, the liquor is strained, and a wineglassful is taken by the afflicted friend each morning for three days. My old gardener says that this remedy always works.

Dick Cutler, Wimborne, 1979

Feverfew

(Chrysanthemum parthenium)

A motorway tea, and a help for migraine sufferers. For the travel-headaches of motorway-driving, a tea made from the flowers or florets of Feverfew is very effective. The flowers

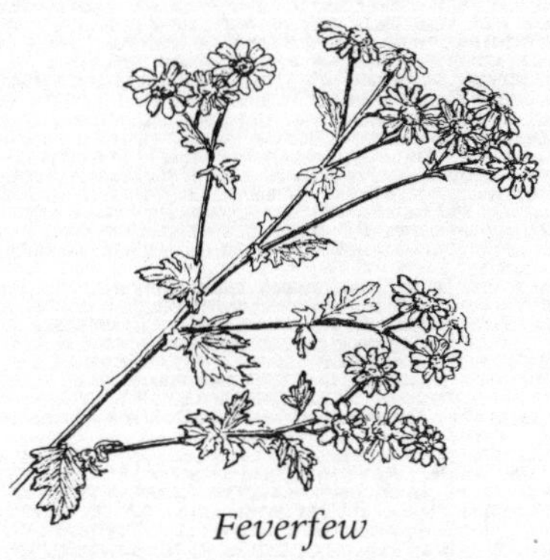

Feverfew

should be gathered and dried as quickly as possible (a sufficient store for a whole year's motorway-driving can be done all at once). The tea is made in the normal way – a four-finger pinch of the dried flowers is sufficient for one headache per person, and as this is a mild sedative, the driver should wait until journey's end for his. Feverfew tea should never be taken in excess.

Roger Banks, 1979

Eyebright

(Euphrasia nemorosa)

Eyebright has been used as an eye medicine for many hundreds of years. It is a neat, firm little plant according to its habitat – on sheep-nibbled downs it will be only an inch and a half high, but when grown unmolested in richer soil it can reach a height of eight inches and looks like a miniature shrub. An infusion of the plant (which should be gathered in July and August) is excellent for inflamed and overworked eyes, and, strained through double linen, the liquor can be used with contact lenses.

Roger Banks, 1979

Meadowsweet

(Filipendula ulmaria)

The creamy, heavily scented curds of the Meadowsweet richly deserve their other country name – 'Queen of the Meadows'. Much used as a strewing herb in former days, it was mingled with the common rushes and the much rarer and more expensive Sweet Flag (*Acorus calamus*), that did duty as floor-covering in former times.

The scent of the Meadowsweet flowers changes after being picked and crushed whereas that of the handsome almond-scented leaves does not. But Meadowsweet is not just a lovely name, an interesting historical herb, a proven herbal remedy of today, and a lingering memory of a walk by a river-bank on a summer evening. Early in the nineteenth century (when it was called 'Spiraea') it was discovered that it contained the same volatile oil and derivatives of salicylic acid that today in chemical form is called aspirin – which means exactly the same thing.

Hart's Tongue Fern

(Phyllitis scolopendrium)

This is the only native Fern to have leaves that look like wet green ribbon. Like most Ferns it

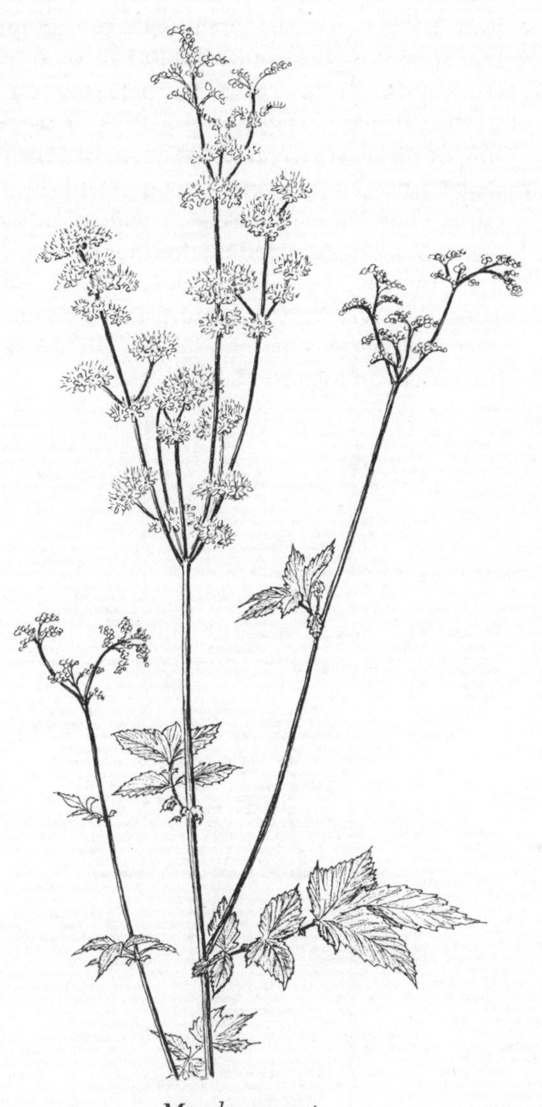

Meadowsweet

likes to grow on the shady side of a country lane, with its toes comfortably in a wet ditch. Hundreds of years ago it was believed to have wonderful contraceptive powers – a piece of the root was worn round the neck, but the root had to be fetched on a moonless night. To-day's knowledge is more practical; an infusion of the leaves is excellent for nephritis, liver disorders, diarrhoea and rheumatism. Hart's Tongue leaves may be found throughout the year, but there is more medicinal virtue in the leaves of summer and early autumn.

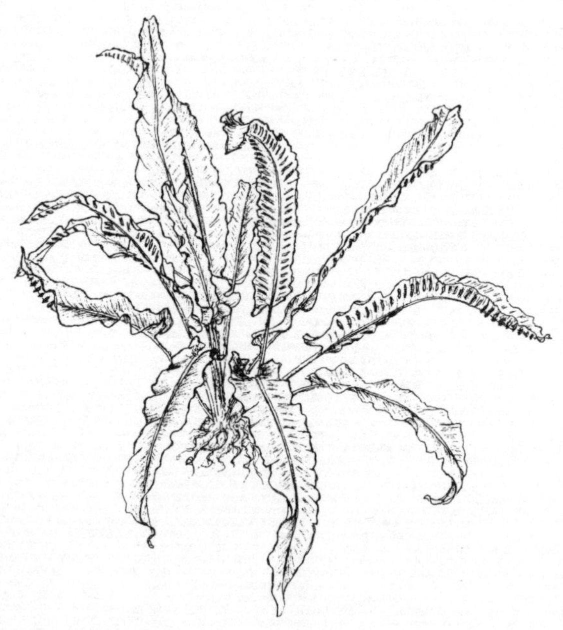

Hart's Tongue

Ivy
(Hedera helix)

Ivy is disliked by most house-owners because it is accused of pulling mortar out of their walls, and by gardeners, because, left to itself, it will suffocate its host-tree. But the plant has many beneficial uses, one among them being this corn-cure. An Ivy leaf should be soaked in lemon juice for three hours, and the sufferer should either have a lengthy hot bath to soften the skin, or soak the affected foot in a bowl of water, changing the water as it will cool more rapidly with the smaller quantity. Bandage the prepared leaf in place, and do the same every day with a fresh leaf. The corn will eventually come away. Throw out the shoes which caused the corn in the first place.

5 Practical Plants

There is a re-awakening and therefore reassuring interest in the plants and trees about us and a growing dislike for the ersatz and the synthetic. So many of the things that grow wild in the country were once used for something useful, and it is fascinating to find out just what one can do with even the most noxious and pestilential weed, let alone the more beautiful plants, flowers and trees. There is a great deal of pleasure to be had in using a nuisance-plant for a practical and useful purpose.

Horsetail

(Equisetum arvense)

This pestilential weed, a vegetable relic of time before man, is so detested that nobody has any hesitation or sentiment about hauling it out of the ground in handfuls (which it will resist); but it does serve two very useful purposes.

First, it can be used as a gentle but very effective saucepan-scourer (do not throw the handful used on to the compost-heap – a piece may escape and re-root). It was formerly used as a natural sander-polisher by cabinet-makers, costing nothing and being readily available for most of the year; dried Horsetail is equally effective in the winter.

A second use for it is as a foliar-food for

Roses, because it excretes a substance which will combat mildew, and Mint- and Hollyhock-rust if sprayed regularly. For this spray take two large handfuls of the green plant, put into a large pan and add enough cold water to cover. Bring to the boil slowly, turn the heat as low as possible and simmer for about twenty minutes with the lid on. Set aside in a cool place for twenty-four hours and then strain. Use this as the concentrate and dilute with two parts water to one of the concentrate.

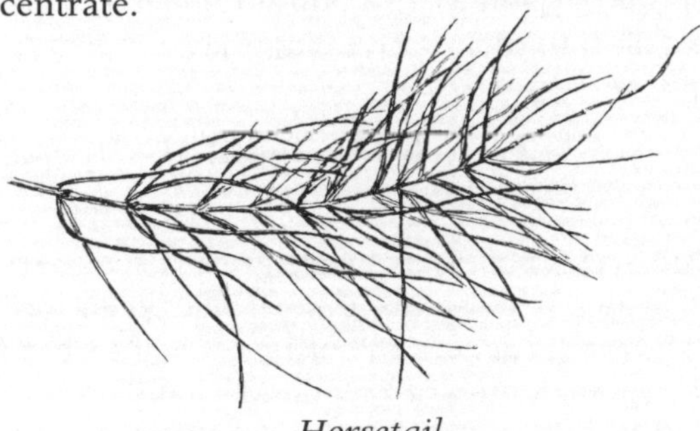

Horsetail

Pyrethrum

(Pyrethrum cinerariaefolium)

This species of the old-fashioned Daisy-flower is the source of the only natural insecticide which is environmentally safe. The flowers of the ordinary garden varieties of Pyrethrum are not as suitable, though they are much prettier.

The plant is grown in Southern Europe, and when the flowers are ready they are harvested at various stages, dried, and ground into powder. To test the quality of the powder that you are buying, catch some house-flies (or a clutch of evil aphis already clustering under the first Rosebuds) and put them in an inverted jam jar with a teaspoonful of the Pyrethrum powder. The insects should be stupified in a minute or so if the powder is fresh, whereas inferior or adulterated powder will take up to half an hour to work.

The plants prefer a dry, free-draining (even gravelly) soil in full sun, and do not thrive in wet English summers; drought conditions in this country suit them admirably, being somewhat akin to their native Yugoslavia.

French Marigold

(Tagetes patula)

Quite accidentally, as many great discoveries are made, it was found by some keen and observant gardeners on both sides of the Channel that an edging of French Marigolds round the vegetable plot kept everything within their circle healthy and disease-free. It was not until recently, however, after considerable research was done, that it was discovered that the roots of the French Marigold excrete a substance which kills soil nematodes (a minute and troublesome worm).

French Marigolds are the hardiest and easiest of plants to grow, and they provide a continuous succession of flowers for months. If they are grown in a greenhouse with Tomatoes, the powerful scent of the Tomato flowers and the Marigolds together will repel white fly.

Chamomile

(Anthemis nobilis)

There are several types of Chamomile, all of which are used medicinally to a greater or lesser degree, but the one which possesses the most virtue is the perennial Chamomile, *Anthemis nobilis*. This is a plant which likes to grow in hot dry conditions in sandy soil, and it makes a delightful path in a small herb-garden, as long as the wear on it is not too heavy. There is a new type of this Chamomile which has been bred for lawn-making which is flowerless and therefore labour-saving.

The whole plant is so health-giving and beneficial in its presence that if a herb, or indeed any garden perennial is ailing, Chamomile should be planted close beside it. After a few weeks it will be noticed that the sick plant is healthier, but the Chamomile should be left in place until the end of the summer until the invalid has recovered, hence Chamomile's other name, 'the Doctor in the Herb-bed'. Chamomile should always be most carefully transplanted, to avoid damage to its own roots, and should preferably be moved during a shower of rain – which is the only safe time to move plants in the summer. Plant Doctor Chamomile on the sunniest side of the sick plant, and if more than one Chamomile plant is likely to be needed it is better to pot them up early in the year to avoid as much root disturbance as possible. The perennial form sends out short 'runners' when established, so a team of Nurses can be kept ready mobilized in pots.

Wild Strawberry

(Fragraria vesca)

This is another well-named plant because the scent of the little scarlet fruits is the essence of fragrant edibility.

Wild Strawberries make a good dentifrice: clean the teeth with the juice of the fruit and leave unrinsed on the teeth for five minutes, which is in itself a pleasure. Then rinse the mouth with a glass of warm water in which a pinch of bicarbonate of soda has been dissolved; this will quite ruin the ambrosial taste of the Strawberry juice, but will leave the teeth shining white.

Garlic

(Allium sativum)

Keep Garlic until it sprouts and then plant the separate cloves on the sunniest side of the rose-bed. This will serve two purposes: the presence of the growing Garlic among the Rose's roots will make the Rose scents stronger, and the growing Garlic exudes a substance that greenfly detest.

Ivy

(Hedera helix)

Ivy is a good stain-remover for navy and black wool garments such as uniforms. Gather a large saucepanful of Ivy leaves, cover with cold water and bring to the boil; this is where you will find that you have put in too many

Ivy leaves – throw some of them away. The pan should be an old iron or enamel one, *not* aluminium. Keep the contents boiling for half an hour, lower the heat and simmer for a further three hours. Cool, strain and measure the liquid remaining, adding a teaspoonful of ammonia to one pint of the liquid. Put this liquid into a labelled bottle and use to remove stains from gabardine, serge, barathea and similar fabrics – but they must be made of 100 per cent wool.

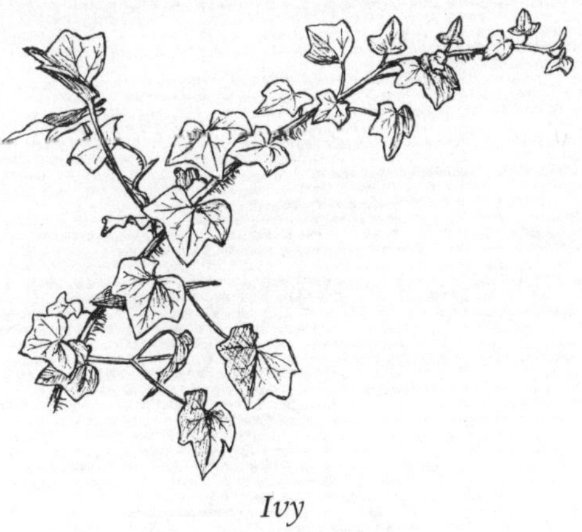

Ivy

Stinging Nettle

(Urtica dioica)

A little-known use for Stinging Nettles is as a beneficial rinse for hair that still retains its natural colour, which it will brighten and improve. A course of rinses will clear dandruff.

Wearing gloves, gather a large handful of the dangling flower-strings and tip them into an enamel saucepan, adding a pint of cold water (for long hair, make double or treble the quantity). Heat slowly over a very low flame until nearly boiling, then watch over the pan for three or four minutes *not* allowing the contents to boil, though the lid of the saucepan should be kept on (this requires a little practice). Remove from the stove and allow to cool naturally overnight, covering with a clean cloth until cold and then replacing the saucepan lid. The clear liquid remaining is the final hair rinse, which should not be strained until just before use.

Nettle

Index